DEPRESSED
TO
HAPPY

Remembering who you are is the
medicine that heals.

CHARLIE GREIG

PREFACE

I find myself embarking on this new project on day 16 of the Coronavirus lockdown in the UK. We haven't yet faced what I know is still to come but you will know better the outcome of the new world, depending on when you are reading this book!

The atmosphere is unlike anything we have ever known. The streets are empty; people seem to be doing their best by putting on a brave face. The British are renowned for this, but in my experience this level of trauma will leave many people scared, adrift, looking for answers to soothe wounds and scars.

This is for whom I am writing this book. I am here to teach, heal and inspire you.

I will do my very best to answer your questions in advance of your asking because I've walked this path already and know how to direct you to finding authentic happiness in a matter of weeks. It's not difficult. You just have to dedicate some time to this and have the courage to be ready for change, to experience an abundant and happy life.

The world is waking up. We can no longer sustain productive and happy lives being governed by fear. It's time for much needed change. The new world is very much on her way. All we have to do is get ready to fully experience the magnificence of what is yet to come.

We are all born with a gift, something that no one else can do. I discovered mine late on in life, but it's never too late to find out what you are born to do and take the appropriate steps towards this. Midlife, in particular, is a time where we begin to question everything we have done and what we want to do for the rest of our lives, so if you are reading this because you are stuck and this is where you are, breathe... It's going to be ok. You are in good hands!

You will learn more about my personal journey as we progress, but in a nutshell, I became totally trapped in fear after a series of life events turned my world upside down, inside out and back to front. I became broken, hopeless and suicidal. This, in hindsight, happened in its own perfect time. If I hadn't experienced these really difficult times, I wouldn't have undertaken 35,000 +

hours of study and practice to now be able to teach people from all walks of life to WAKE UP.

So what does WAKING UP mean?

In a spiritual sense, it means learning to exist at a higher state of consciousness, to understand who you are, what you are here to do and how. This is achieved by mastering a number of steps. Nothing ever worth having comes easily and connection with self is no exception, but there is a prize at the end of all this learning. You will be calm, grateful, loving, kind, forgiving, purposeful and no longer be governed by fear. In other words, HAPPY.

To demonstrate this in terms of a physical feeling, if you consider the feeling you get when you are hopelessly in LOVE being a number 2 on a scale of 1-5, being fully conscious would rank at number 5 when you come into full soul consciousness.

I will call this "AUTHENTIC".

I appreciate not everyone is ready to awaken spiritually at this time. This is a choice we make before we come to earth to have a physical experience, so my aim for this book is to keep it practical, more worldly and easier to follow.

If you want a more spiritual experience, you can always follow my ON DEMAND video programme of 10 lessons available at www.whoamilondon.com.

What I can promise you is if you are feeling like life has collapsed around you for whatever reason, and you can't see a way out, if you do the work outlined in this book you will feel significantly better. You will no longer be trapped in fear, you will understand your purpose, and you will feel empowered, clear and in flow.

This state of flow is delicious and creates an abundant life.

Our birth right is to live an abundant and happy life. You don't have to be rich or famous to experience this, you just have to change the way you look at things and when you do, guess what, the things you look at change.

It is my absolute pleasure to take you on this incredible journey of discovery to help you AWAKEN and find the life of bliss you desire.

Lets begin...

I dedicate this book to all the souls who are caring for the world at this time in whatever guise. You are greatly appreciated.

We all have a part to play in this historic worldly event to ensure the new world reflects who we are to become.

The Teacher.

CONTENTS

Work through the chapters in numerical order as they have been designed to lift you in a specific sequence.

INTRODUCTION

Firstly, I want to commend you for taking action. Getting to this first step takes great courage to make change when times are tough. I know, I've been there!

My story relevant to this book began in 2010. I had amassed millions of pounds building bespoke properties for clients and myself.

I invested everything I had in a brilliant modular housing system, Cub, that was launched at least a decade before it's time. I am always too early! Needless to say, I became bankrupt, penniless and totally broken.

I couldn't see a way out. I sat in "Poor Me" for at least two years until enough was enough. It was do or die time literally!

In a second, life really can change.

I typed WHO AM I into Google and the POWER OF NOW appeared. This was the beginning of my journey. I was ready to discover whom I was and what I was here to do, to rebuild my life at the age of 50.

The next five years flew by. I studied everyday, I became a Master but more importantly I identified the formula for authentic happiness.

I now teach full time and absolutely love it. To see the transformation in people in a matter of weeks is so rewarding. It makes every ounce of pain and suffering I went through worth it.

I teach people HAPPY. Who wouldn't love to do that as a job!

The knowledge you are going to digest and practise over the coming weeks or months will change your life forever. You will be amazed at how the mind dominates our experience, it basically runs the show!

THE MIND IS NOT WHO YOU ARE.

Learning how to live in the moment fully is a game changer, you escape the mind completely, and you become free of depression and anxiety.

This step takes practice but I will share some wonderful techniques.

Establishing purpose is one of the most empowering exercises you can do.

Are you doing what you came to do?

When you are in discord with your purpose, frustration and anger become dominant forces ruining your physical experience. When you find purpose, you find flow.

Becoming a grateful master is paramount to changing how you see the world. When you exist in gratitude, and this is a physical and emotional feeling, you are released from the mind allowing you to operate from a place of "authentic." Decisions become clearer and are based on LOVE.

I know from being in "Poor Me", I wasn't grateful for anything. Life sucked and I didn't want to be here. At the time this felt right, but when I realised everything is energy and that like attracts like, if you are putting out "Poor Me" into the universe, it's going to send this back to you straight away, so be careful what you are asking for. If you feel like you're on a constant wheel of repeat, consider what your negative daily thought is then turn that around. Is that what you are experiencing?

Try from today to replace negative with positive thoughts as a start to this process.

We carry so much regret and spite with us accumulated throughout life. It's like being shackled with weights around your ankles till you can't move. You have to let it go. I have some beautiful techniques to help with this.

I'll show you how to get round the mind so it can't get involved!

You will feel your vibration rise as you work through the steps I outline. Again, this is a physical feeling. It's like an internal level of water that rises and sinks depending on how you are working with your emotions. We have a choice in every moment. When out of balance we don't choose "positive" because being negative is far more familiar. The problem with this is our energy/vibration attracts exactly what we don't want.

LIKE UNTO ITSELF IS DRAWN.

It's a bit like fear attracts fear, which is what is occurring now.

When you learn to sustain a higher vibration, life changes. It feels like your luck has changed. The ultimate goal is contentment. This state requires no energy; it is a state of being that just IS. The more focussed and managed your vibration is, the more quickly manifestations appear into your life.

In many cases, it's just because you are looking, anticipating and attracting...

AGAIN, LIKE UNTO ITSELF IS DRAWN.

Are you beginning to see a pattern here!

There are so many facets to finding this place of happiness but we are going to work through the steps in the right order and cement new foundations and beliefs. I'm so excited for you as I type this, as I know how you will feel when you complete all these steps. The new world will require new ways.

I would highly recommend purchasing a journal, about 200 pages, a good size that you can use throughout this process. In each chapter I will provide tasks to do at home. Keeping a journal is also an essential process of allowing and surrender, so buy one you like that you will enjoy using every day. Your journal is your private therapist. I recommend keeping your journal going for the foreseeable future as a habit not to be broken. It's wonderful to check on your own progress in the coming weeks and months ahead.

If you are an all or nothing type of person like me, you may want to read the whole book and then go back and do the steps. This is not just a read book. I would highly recommend doing the exercises to see amazing changes appear in your life.

So, are we ready?

Shall we take you to a place you never knew existed?

Shall we get you happy?

Lets do this...

POOR ME

TAKE RESPONSIBILITY FOR YOURSELF.

I'm afraid the days of "Poor Me" have to cease, this mindset is sabotaging your life.

From day one you have to take your power back, wherever your power has strayed to. Make some adjustments in your work and private life to help you do this. It's always better to tell people if you are making life changes, people cannot know what you are thinking. We are going to cover this in more detail later, but be kind and open, treat others the way you would like to be treated and see what happens.

This is a good thing, be excited.

Self love is something everyone struggles with, it's not what we are used to. We go through our whole lives trying to be good humans by pleasing others, but perhaps when you look at this from a higher perspective, you may see this as fuelling consumerism. Happiness cannot be bought in any store.

If you picture your LOVE cup being a vessel in your chest area, close your eyes and feel how full this is?

EMPTY?

Not surprised, but that's ok. We have plenty of room to fill it up!

Go back regularly and check on this and notice how the level is rising as you go through this process.

SELF-LOVE IS PRACTISED IN A NUMBER OF WAYS.

Meditation, fitness, reading, healthy eating, bubble baths, good practice and creativity are recommended. Basically, anything you do for you that make's you feel good.

Creating a routine helps bypass the mind that will defiantly tell you not to bother today!

Keep a tidy and healthy home. Keep your fridge filled with colourful and nutritious food. There is no point cleaning the inner you if the outer you is not in alignment. Give up drugs and alcohol and cigarettes if you can. All stimulants lower your vibration and keep you asleep. It doesn't have to be forever, but we need to get you into balance and then you can gently introduce a level you are happy with. It's all about balance.

If you are on antidepressants, see how you feel in a few weeks and perhaps speak to your GP about reducing and slowly coming off these. I am not a doctor; I'm a teacher so please follow the advice of your GP.

CHAKRAS

Maintaining your chakras is vital to good energy and flow. There are over 30,000 but we will just look at 7. If you imagine these are balls of energy located at positions within your body, supporting areas of your body, all in tune with each other and vibrating, this will be good enough for now. Coloured food groups stimulate the corresponding chakra, so diet is important when you are becoming brighter.

These are also good indicators of health.

Meditation helps you monitor your internal body; the internal body needs TLC too.

Below are details on the 7 chakras and the colours and organs associated with these?

Make a note in your journal of particular chakras where you identify many ailments. These need to be worked on. I'll explain how.

Root - Red
Sacral - Orange
Solar Plexus - Yellow
Heart - Green
Throat - Blue
Third eye - Violet
Crown – White

Chakras are located throughout our body. Each chakra correlates to specific body ailments and physical dysfunctions. Each energy centre also houses our mental and emotional strengths. When we have a physical issue, it creates weaknesses in our emotional behaviour. When we release the stale energy from the body, it can undo any tightness, stiffness or malfunction of that area.

The clearing of the energy can also balance our emotional state of mind. The Chakra Mind-Body Balance is a two-way street; if there are certain fears and emotions we are holding on to, we experience physical restrictions too.

If you have achiness or stiffness or certain recurring emotions and fears, read on and you will find out which chakra is affected or blocked.

1ST OR ROOT CHAKRA

Located at the base of your spine, at your tailbone.

Physical imbalances in the root chakra include problems in the legs, feet, rectum, tailbone, immune system, male reproductive parts and prostate gland. Those with imbalances here are also likely to experience issues of degenerative arthritis, knee pain, sciatica, eating disorders and constipation.

Emotional imbalances include feelings affecting our basic survival needs - money, shelter and food - the ability to provide for life's necessities.

When this chakra is balanced, you feel supported, grounded with a sense of connection and safety to the physical world.

THE LESSON OF THIS CHAKRA IS SELF-PRESERVATION; WE HAVE A RIGHT TO BE HERE.

2ND OR SACRAL CHAKRA

Located two inches below your navel. Physical imbalances include sexual and reproductive issues, urinary problems, kidney dysfunctions, hip, pelvic and lower back pain.

Emotional imbalances include our commitment to relationships, our ability to express our emotions, our ability to have fun, play based on desires, creativity, pleasure and sexuality. Fear of impotence, betrayal and addictions.

When this chakra is balanced, we have the ability to take risks, we are creative, and we are committed, passionate, sexual and outgoing.

THE LESSON OF THIS CHAKRA IS TO HONOUR YOURSELF AND OTHERS.

3RD OR SOLAR PLEXUS CHAKRA

Located three inches above your navel.

Physical imbalances include digestive problems, liver dysfunction, chronic fatigue, high blood pressure, diabetes, stomach ulcers, pancreatic and gall bladder issues, and colon diseases.

Emotional imbalances include issues of personal power and self-esteem; our inner critic comes out. Fear of rejection, criticism, and physical appearances.

When this chakra is balanced, we feel self-respect and self-compassion.

We feel in control, assertive, confident.

THE LESSON OF THIS CHAKRA IS SELF-ACCEPTANCE.

4TH OR HEART CHAKRA

Located in the centre of the chest.

Physical imbalances include asthma, heart disease, lung disease, issues with breasts, lymphatic systems, upper back and shoulder problems, arm and wrist pain.

Emotional imbalances include issues of the heart; over loving to the point of suffocation, jealousy, abandonment, anger, and bitterness. Fear of loneliness.

When this chakra is balanced, we feel joy, gratitude, love and compassion. Forgiveness flows freely, and trust is gained.

THE LESSON OF THIS CHAKRA IS I LOVE.

5TH OR THROAT CHAKRA

Located at the throat.

Physical imbalances include thyroid issues, sore throats, laryngitis, TMJ, ear infections, ulcers, any facial problems (chin, cheek, lips, tongue problems) neck and shoulder pain.

Emotional imbalances include issues of self-expression through communication, both spoken or written. Fear of no power or choice.

No willpower or being out of control.

When this chakra is balanced, we have free flow of words, expression, and communication. We are honest and truthful yet firm. We are good listeners.

THE LESSON OF THIS CHAKRA IS TO SPEAK UP AND LET YOUR VOICE BE HEARD.

6TH OR THIRD EYE CHAKRA

Located in the middle of the eyebrows, in the centre of the forehead.

Physical imbalances include headaches, blurred vision, sinus issues, eyestrain, seizures, hearing loss and hormone function.

Emotional imbalances include issues with moodiness, volatility, and self-reflection; an inability to look at one's own fears and to learn from others.

We daydream often and live in a world with exaggerated imagination.

When this chakra is balanced, we feel clear, focused and can determine between truth and illusion. We are open to receiving wisdom and insight.

THE LESSON OF THIS CHAKRA IS TO SEE THE BIG PICTURE.

7TH OR CROWN CHAKRA

Located at the top of the head.

Physical imbalances include depression, inability to learn, sensitivity to light, sound and environment.

Emotional imbalances include issues with self-knowledge and greater power. Imbalances arise from rigid thoughts on religion and spirituality, constant confusion and you will overanalyse everything until you are paralysed. Fear of alienation.

When this chakra is balanced, we live in the present moment. We have an unshakable trust in our inner guidance.

THE LESSON OF THIS CHAKRA IS LIVE MINDFULLY.

The best way to start balancing the chakras is to start at the root chakra and work your way up to the crown chakra. You may feel that more than one chakra is imbalanced or blocked. This is because when one is blocked, the other chakras begin to compensate and either become overactive or underactive. I recommend going into meditation. Start at the root chakra and visualise all of the chakras one by one, spinning healthily and strong. If any are not spinning, just activate them with the mind. Take your time and do this exercise with loving intention. You are healing your internal self.

Make a note in your journal of any chakras that you feel are blocked.

Support these with the colour associated with this chakra by eating food that matches in colour. Be aware of the food/medicine as you ingest it, the body will then gratefully accept it and put it to work for your highest good.

It's all about connection and belief.

GRATITUDE IS ONE OF THE KEY STEPS TO LIVING A FULFILLED AND HAPPY LIFE.

When you exist in gratitude, even for the bad stuff, you see things in a different way, from the heart. Gratitude starts today. Make a list in your journal. What are you grateful for in your life right now?

Keep it basic, roof over your head, food, security and family...

If one of these doesn't apply, put in what you do have in your life.

PLEASE REMEMBER... YOU ARE NOT WHAT YOU HAVE. YOU ARE WHAT YOU HAVE CHOSEN TO BE.

Watch the mind here, it will get involved. Just focus on the heart centre and hold your energy there. The mind cannot get involved here. Feel the heat and tingly sensation when you do this; you are beginning to connect to your internal self.

BE GRATEFUL FOR THIS TOO!

When you start seeing what you already have in your life, you start feeling safe and in appreciation. Notice every day how blessed you are and enjoy these things to fill up your LOVE cup!

I would recommend keeping your gratitude list topped up and visit this regularly. Everyone on earth is becoming more grateful for things we once took for granted. Even a walk in the park!!

TIME TO LOOK IN THE MIRROR.

We rarely look at ourselves with love when we look in the mirror.

We look to see if our bum looks big, if we have clean teeth or as a glance of reassurance as we leave home, but we very rarely take time to look into our eyes and take time to enquire, see, feel and love who we are. I would recommend a full-length mirror if possible so you don't cut your Chi energy and take some time to see/feel who you really are.

WITH LOVE

The body is a miraculous machine. It does everything for us in perfect rhythm. We often don't appreciate good health until we don't have it.

Your mirror can also be used to write your affirmations on too if you wish.

As we have discussed, everything is energy, vibration, so everything has a frequency. Pictures, words, colours and sounds all have a vibrational value.

So, it would make sense to surround your full length mirror with pictures of when you were truly happy, with people you love that were and are in your life, poems that stir your soul, mother's day cards from your little ones, whatever you like. Dig out pictures and items that make you feel loved and happy and attach these all around your mirror.

The point of this is when you stand looking at yourself or doing your daily affirmations, you are surrounded with a love vibration that is YOURS. You are no longer alone. If you understand the concept that everything is energy, including us, how could you ever be alone? We are all connected.

This has a profound effect on your wellbeing and helps you practice further gratitude.

DEVICES

I highly recommend detoxing from your phone while you start this journey. The reason why phones are so bad for your mental wellbeing is that they keep you trapped to the material world, which is governed by ego/fear. You compare yourself to other people who are probably better off or more famous than you which is why you are attracted to them in the first place, but all this does is leave you feeling unworthy and depleted.

Even I limit myself to half an hour a day for Social Media, any more and I can feel my vibration lowering. Most of what you see is FAKE anyway so use your time more productively especially in the first few weeks of your journey.

JOURNALING

We touched on this earlier. I would recommend making journaling a habit every morning or evening, whichever suits your lifestyle.

Ask yourself questions like, "How can tomorrow be better than today? What did I do brilliantly today? Or what growth was established today?"

I have kept a journal for over 5 years.

I could never have built my programme without the knowledge that was documented in these.

It was like putting a jigsaw of gorgeousness together.

It's beautiful to look back and review how much you have grown.

DE CLUTTER YOUR HOME.

Give to charity anything you no longer need and ensure you do this with joy rather than resentment. Give to those that have less than you and really notice how lucky you are compared to so many and how grateful they are to receive your kind donations. If you are working on your internal self, your immediate surrounding must also be clear of clutter, free flowing, enticing and necessary.

LOVE your home.

LAST BUT NOT LEAST, MEDITATION.

Daily practice of meditation is a routine that also needs to be mastered. Learning to be still, to find this inner place of joy, to give time to you to just be, is key to feeling mentally, physically and spiritually well.

This is also how you higher your vibration and align and find inner peace.

Your practice should be something that you consider as a wonderful necessity, time for you. As you get more into the flow, you will receive inspiration and messages.

I do a wonderful meditation as part of my ON DEMAND video programme, but there are so many to choose from on YouTube. Try a few and find what you like. This is your journey, design it as you wish.

THE AFFIRMATION I RECOMMEND TO START WITH IS:

I AM POWERFUL AND I AM LOVING,

I AM POWERFUL AND I AM LOVED,

I AM POWERFUL AND I LOVE IT.

Write this on your I LOVE YOU or bathroom mirror and say this 11 times morning and evening while looking into your eyes. Drink in the empowerment that comes with this and feel your LOVE cup start filling. You will be keeping this affirmation going for the next 4 weeks.

So, to close on week one. Well Done! You have a lot of work to do getting yourself ready for some life-changing lessons to come.

These points might sound basic but they work. I use these and similar techniques with my private clients.

I wish you love on this first step of your journey.

Keep busy and watch the mind. Observe your thoughts this week. How much time are you spending being negative? Just observe for now and try and keep positive thoughts predominant.

THE MIND

How are you doing?

Are you meditating every day, keeping your journal, living in a brighter and happier home? Have you DE cluttered your home, kept your diet healthy and become more aware of feeding your body energetically?

What has the mind been telling you? Have you managed to turn negative thoughts into positive? How brilliant are you feeling when you stand in front of your I LOVE YOU mirror? Feeling less alone, more hopeful?

GREAT

In this chapter we are looking and working with the mind.

The mind is so powerful it can kill the host. Balance is key.

Imagine a brain, about the size of a small football with two sides. This is relevant throughout my teaching.

LEFT-BRAIN IS DOMINATED BY EGO/FEAR, AND RIGHT BRAIN IS FOCUSED ON CREATIVITY AND HIGHER SELF.

The aim is to exercise right brain to the point that it is fully firing. Left-brain becomes quieter, only to be used for practical functions similar to a satnav or computer.

If you imagine an elastic band wound very tightly on the left, you can imagine the force the right hand side would feel. This is what it's like when you are depressed; you get pulled to the left and you become dominated by ego and fear.

Ego is a false personality chosen by you to prevent you from dying.

Ego wants to keep you safe, but there is safe and there is paralysed!

READ THIS FIRST AND THEN DO THIS VISUALISATION.

Hold your focus behind your right eye. Imagine this as a spinning ball of white bright energy, and hold this firmly in position. Now holding it there, try and think of something negative.

You can't. You can feel the left hand brain pulling you back. It's like a slider; you can feel the difference between left and right hand brain.

The work is to stay in right hand brain as much as possible. This is like going to a brain gym! By constantly focusing on this you are strengthening this muscle, opening new connections, becoming more who you are.

It's not always easy when we are feeling sad or anxious to think positive thoughts. I get this. It's more familiar to stay in a place that you know, but this work has to be done to get you back in balance, so I recommend this little rift...

If you are thinking negative thoughts, flip it. Say, "Wouldn't it be wonderful if..." then add your part... "Someone bought me a coffee, my train came on time" or in my case at present, to be allowed outside!

Keep doing this and start feeling the difference in your wellbeing.

I work on the emotional scale to assess where clients are at the beginning of their journey.

THERE ARE 22 EMOTIONS.

1. Joy/Knowledge/Empowerment/ Freedom/
2. Love/Appreciation
3. Passion
4. Enthusiasm/Eagerness/ Happiness
5. Positive Expectation/Belief
6. Optimism
7. Hopefulness
8. Contentment
9. Boredom
10. Pessimism
11. Frustration/Irritation/Impatience
12. Feeling Overwhelmed
13. Disappointment
14. Doubt
15. Worry
16. Blame
17. Discouragement
18. Anger
19. Revenge
20. Hatred/Rage
21. Jealousy
22. Insecurity/Guilt/Unworthiness
23. Fear/Grief/Depression/Despair/
24. Powerlessness

Where are you on this scale?

You will probably be between two numbers. Make a note of this in your journal so you can see the improvement in a few weeks.

Imagine this as a road. To the left, it's muddy and dark and non-inviting. At number 7, hopefulness, there is a bridge HOME and beyond that to number 1 is sunshine, love, joy and definitely where you want to be heading!

Stand on this bridge. Feel how secure and safe this is. You can clearly see how uninviting it is to the left. You can feel the warmth of the emotions on the right.

This is home for you from now on. Whenever you're off balance, get back to the bridge using the rift I gave you or through sheer willpower through positivity. This work is so important to your wellness. Don't underestimate the power of what I'm sharing. The first few steps I share are life changing. You move up a level, you start feeling separation from the mind.

PLEASE WORK ON THIS STEP ALL WEEK WITH FULL INTENT. Stay mindful.

As we are working on the mind this week and what the mind tells us, we need to look closely at who is the voice in your head. We are not who we think we are.

READ THIS, AND THEN DO THIS VISUALISATION.

Close your eyes. Imagine you are in an empty cinema, it's dark, you are there alone, it's safe and you are excited about what you are going to see.   Sit down in the back row, and project whatever thoughts you like as a movie onto the screen.   Let the mind do its thing, become an observer of the mind, see how jumbled and random thoughts are. Notice the flavour of the tone, become engrossed in the movie of you. When you are ready, come back into the room.

DO NOT READ BELOW UNTIL YOU HAVE FINISHED THIS VISUALISATION.

Now. Who was the person sitting in the back of the cinema?

The observer with higher wisdom and presence.

This is your authentic self. This is the voice you need to operate from. It's about love, beauty, truth, compassion, authenticity, wisdom, and higher consciousness. Part of everything that is, you are not alone.

So now we know the mind is FAKE, you should find it easier to do the work this week. It doesn't matter if you don't feel like being positive. DO IT. It's for a function to strengthen your right hand brain, which I promise you is key to becoming authentically happy. Baby steps. The more you do this, the easier it becomes. You can restart in any moment.

Fear is gripping the world at present. Mother Nature is helping us by creating time for reflection to help us remember who we are. We must learn to replace fear with LOVE. A new world will not be visible in all its glory to those who cannot see.

MAKE A LIST IN YOUR JOURNAL OF 5 THINGS YOU ARE FEARFUL OF.

Under each one write why and how you are going to overcome these.

Baby steps are always better and you will discover that these will melt away naturally, but document them anyway for future reading so you can see how far you are progressing.

We have a choice in every moment. Make the choice of happiness, growth, dedication to self, love for one another, and be grateful and kind.

What we emit is what we attract. Notice how more people are reacting to you. Look people in the eye, become assertive, you are powerful, you are a beautiful being of light and love.

You are beginning to remember who you are and others can feel this.

3

THIS MOMENT

I trust that last week's lesson was an eye opener and that you are beginning to see the truth emerging. How could we have been living in a world that is not what we thought it was for so long!

This step is HUGE. You will have read in the preface that, "The Power of Now" by Eckhart Tolle literally saved my life. I would highly recommend you read this if you haven't already. Life changing. Thank you Eckhart.

I couldn't see because I was only focused on the past and the future, living in regret and pain and doubt and worry.

When you remain in this very moment with Zen like focus, the past, which is depression and the future, which is anxiety cannot exist.

Ask yourself. Is everything ok in this moment? You are breathing, the sun is shining, you have food in your tummy.

YES. Then everything is perfect.

If it is not, change something so that it is.

The more we can sit in what troubles us, the more growth we achieve.

I will show you a technique for this later on.

WHAT IS LIVING IN THE MOMENT?

It's becoming completely absorbed in this moment using all your senses, sight, smell, taste, touch and hearing. When you activate these, you step into a totally focused state of being. The middle way.

Sit quietly and just see what you can feel, smell, touch, hear and taste. Put your mind to work documenting all of these feelings. Notice how alive you are, your heartbeat, the feeling of clothes touching your skin, the odour in the air, the temperature of the environment. Drink it in.

This realisation is best practised in nature. The vibration is already high, there are so many beautiful things to see and we also get chance to breathe.

When you practise this in nature, focus on how your heart expands. You get a warm and sometimes emotional feeling of overwhelming joy. This is how life should feel in every moment.

You will also notice the mind did not interrupt you!

THIS IS LIVING IN THE MOMENT.

Once you have felt this, you won't want to ever feel like you did before.

Practise. Practise. Practise.

BE PRESENT.

You will hear me say this many times throughout this book, "The joy is in the journey". You have to appreciate every step and stay present to be released from the mind. If you are present, you are in joy, it's that simple.

The mind cannot focus on two emotions at the same time.

Choose JOY every time.

The more time you stay present, the happier you will feel. The more you do it, the more the habit forms. Doing this work is not easy but what could be more important than this!

I can't tell you how grateful I am to have mastered this skill. I can imagine how people are feeling right now in this pandemic. The news feeds the ego, the ego reacts and holds you safe and the cycle repeats.

Whatever era you are in when reading this, ESCAPE FEAR, it's your only work.

Baby steps are the best here; take one moment at a time. Yes, we have hopes and dreams but let's come to those in a while. Let's master this life-changing step first and everything will become clearer.

IF YOU ARE FOCUSED ON THE THERE YOU ARE MISSING THE HERE.

Another important step here when you are out and about smelling the roses, smiling at people, seeing nature and architecture in its full glory, remember to keep your eyes off the pavement. As soon as you look down, the mind takes over. You will see this in people who are insane. The mind is not only dominant internally but the mouth articulates the mind's story. Keep your head up and see the beautiful world we have been gifted to live in.

BE IN PRESENT GRATITUDE.

The other benefits of mastering this step is food tastes better, sleep is better, calmness is felt, beauty is seen, life becomes delicious.

It's easier to tackle difficult tasks in this state of presence. Become what it is, higher your vibration to influence the atmosphere, stay alert from a place of kindness, make that moment a moment of bliss. War and fighting, greed and blame are all low energy emotions and will become your dominant force if you allow this.

Be light, be YOU.

LIKE UNTO ITSELF IS DRAWN.

Just a quick reminder! What you put out there will come back to you in a matched vibration. Invite what you want with how you interact, think and behave.

When you master this and you may get to see this the first time you do this in nature, you will see in technicolour, colours seem brighter, sounds more prominent, smells more pronounced, feelings more enhanced. The veil of forgetfulness is lifting.

The world we once saw is no longer what we see.

YOU ARE WAKING UP.

4

ESTABLISHING PURPOSE

How's life looking? Keeping up good practice? Feeling better?

GREAT.

The question I mostly get asked during my work as a teacher is, "What is my purpose?" Establishing purpose is what helps us get into flow; you get to do what you came to do. When we are not following purpose, we display emotions of anger, unworthiness, regret, hate and many other lower emotions. We feel off balance.

The most wonderful way to find purpose is to have your soul plan chart prepared. You can do this yourself or have me do it. Details are on my website. www.whoamilondon.com. You can prepare your own chart by following the steps in, "Soul Plan" by Blue Marsden which I also highly recommend reading.

Your Soul Plan is a holographic imprint of your soul and is calculated using your birth name. It lets you know what challenges need to be overcome, what talents you possess which should be used to overcome your challenges and what your goals are both worldly and spiritually. The final step is your soul destiny, what is the primary goal for this lifetime. I use my Soul Plan all the time to check where I am and use its direction to steer my ship. There is a huge amount of further learning you can do if you become as fascinated by this as I am.

Soul Plan is based on ancient Hebrew numerology and is the most accurate method I have come across for finding purpose.

I would also highly recommend, "The Life You Were Born To Live" by Dan Millman which uses your birth date to show fairly accurately your traits and personality. I am for example a 22/4, Master Builder. This shows why I spent 30 years building homes and companies and products! Nothing is by accident; your soul directs you through life. You have free will of course so you are free to wander where you wish but if it's time to realign, events will appear to ensure growth is achieved as it did in my case.

I needed to step into the role of Teacher, which is my worldly goal, so the universe very kindly came and pulled the rug from under my feet.

I do have stubbornness as my chief feature!

To work out what your numerology life number is, add all the digits of your birth date together and then add the two numbers in the total to give you the end number.

i.e. 1+0+0+2+1+9+6+3=22

2+2=4 22/4

The first number is our internal challenges, the second number is external challenges and the last number is your goal, what pulls you forward.

Once you understand about this it gives you another level of knowing. You understand why we behave the way we do!

Don't get so wrapped up in the drama of life and what you are told you should do. If you are being pushed in a direction that feels unfamiliar or uncomfortable, try and see the treasure. Are you missing a message that is being sent? Life is a gift and opportunities appear everywhere when we have our eyes open. The universe may want to direct you in a better way, be open to consider and see the bigger picture. Keep your vibration high and put out to the universe exactly who you are and what you want but stay flexible.

Worrying about things is just the mind taking over. It takes a significant amount of energy which is why when you are off balance you are often exhausted. Be vigilant, you know this now. It's just a brilliantly orchestrated game that we have all chosen to play.

THE NEXT STEP TO ESTABLISHING PURPOSE IS TO ASK YOURSELF SOME FUNDAMENTAL QUESTIONS.

Use your journal for this.

ASK YOURSELF:

If money were no object, what would I do in life?

What are my unique talents?

How can I use my unique talents to serve humanity?

What makes me happy?

Give yourself plenty of time to answer these. Some clues will be in your Soul Plan, but you can also reflect on what you liked doing when you were a child. Were you kind and nurturing, did you make things, or did you like to analyse or calculate or read?

There are some big clues to be found in our childhood. As ego doesn't become dominant until mid teens, a purer version of YOU existed then.

The question, "What makes me happy?" is really important.

Any career in life must include what makes you happy. List everything that makes you happy.

This can be anything from sunshine to cups of tea, friends, or locations.

Once you have spent some time working on this you will begin to see a clear indication of purpose. Sometimes your Soul Plan will just say, "You have the ability to become a Profound Spiritual Teacher to teachers of this world and not yet", which was the case in mine, but even if not so specific, it will greatly help you.

Some of us have chosen less structured life plans. Put all elements of what you learn from this chapter and keep working on it till you see a clear picture. It took me six months to do this exercise and I allow 6 weeks with one to one clients, so take your time and enjoy the process.

Only society says you have to have the best-paid job, work long hours all your life till you retire. NO. The soul has a plan. Find out what this is and step into your purpose to find flow.

When you are in flow, it's a little like being in a boat floating downstream with no oars, lying in the sunshine with hands behind your head, in the moment, manifesting what you want, *verses* not in flow which is like facing upstream with no oars, paddling frantically with your hands and getting nowhere.

Sound familiar?

We all choose goals, roles, modes, attitudes, chief features, needs and centres before we come with many, many other choices.

There is a universal plan. Just trust the process.

The old way of thinking didn't bring you any joy did it, so this is the time for change!

Establishing purpose is crucial to your happiness. If you were born to be a gardener and you work as a broker in the city, you are in the wrong job and you will never feel satisfied.

When you enjoy what you do and bring your gift into the world, you feel worthy. You are here doing what you came to do. You are in bliss.

The beauty of doing this work is that you become resistant to the constant barrage of stuff that is being sold to us in every moment of every day, which causes us to feel overwhelmed. We feel more clarity.

We don't need loads of stuff when we discover authentic happiness. We need less money and if we need less money we don't have to work so hard or take a job that doesn't suit who we are. We are happier and attract more of the same. When in flow, your vibration is raised and you exist in a higher state of consciousness.

It can be no other way.

FOR YOUR SANITY AND HAPPINESS, PLEASE MASTER THIS STEP.

FORGIVENESS

We have accomplished so much together already. These first few steps are huge and really help lift you.

How are you feeling?

I'm anticipating, "Much better, thank you". I am so proud of you. It takes great courage to bring about positive change.

In this chapter we are going to look at forgiveness. We have cemented strong foundations already so we can start looking at the demons of the past knowing that they are only emotions triggered by the mind, so we can handle this.

Write down in your journal everything you have to forgive. This can be what you did to others, what they did to you, what you didn't do, whatever it is, put it down in your journal. This may be the first time you see in black and white what is holding you back. Be very gentle with yourself during this process.

After each thing you are listing, leave a space underneath that you can use to discover the treasure. Everything happens for a reason. We have asked other humans to come into our existence for learning. This learning may have required an action of unkindness to establish the most growth, but you will have agreed this with whoever is providing these actions, so let it go, you gave permission!

PAIN IS A WONDERFUL MOTIVATOR, IT MAKES YOU TAKE ACTION.

Decipher what it is you have written down and look into it. What did you gain from that experience? How did it benefit you? What was the treasure?

I'll give you an example. When I was growing up I was in awe of my father. He was a pilot, draughtsman, actor, skipper, highly articulate and had an amazing presence. As the eldest, I tried to master skills to gain recognition as all children do. I didn't get this and it affected me most of my life. I held grudges. How could he not say, "Well done darling!" I was a little girl but actually the treasure is, it made me so determined to achieve what I set out to do and I have completed much learning in this lifetime. Through agreement with him, he gave me exactly what I asked for and needed.

FIND THE TREASURE.

This process may take a while. Keep everything in your journal for the further steps that are to come. Your only work is to **forgive yourself**, to cut the ties with LOVE from the people you are connected to in this conflict.

Let the universe handle the rest. When you truly forgive, you cut any ties with lower energies that were holding you prisoner and you are free to move forward.

Be very aware of the mind during this process, it will present reasons why you shouldn't forgive. Drop into your heart centre and think from there.

Surround yourself with things that make you happy. Treat yourself like a king or queen this week. You are worth it.

Gratitude will also save you this week. Be grateful for the growth you have achieved from each of the things on your list. If you are growing, everything is perfect. The soul is not in a rush as long as you are in forward motion.

BABY STEPS.

"Ho'oponopono" by Luc Bodin, M.D., Nathalie Bodin Lamboy and Jean Graciet is a fabulous book and I highly recommend reading this.

This Hawaiian system of forgiveness is so simple yet so effective. The elders of communities in Hawaii used this system to maintain harmony and kindness in the communities they looked after.

This system is used worldwide and is a wonderful foundation to acquire.

I am bringing in a new affirmation this week. You can continue with, "I am powerful" if you still need it or if you feel like your love cup is FULL then you can replace with this, otherwise do both.

It is...
I am sorry
Please forgive me
Thank you
I love you.
THE "YOU" IS SAID TO YOURSELF
Like before, say this affirmation looking into your soul through your eyes, drinking in the words and forgive yourself. Do this morning and

evening, about 11 times, more if you feel like. Repetition is key. We are building new habits. Some people struggle with "I love you" keep trying, you will allow this after a few times. Focus on your LOVE cup and drink this in.

The importance of forgiveness cannot be underestimated. Why would you want to carry regret and pain into your future? We exist in the NOW so there is no place for old baggage here. Nothing that ever happened to you has affected the essence of you. You are bright, love, energy. Outdated memories trigger emotions and cause pain. If you have cut the ties and let it all go, you will no longer feel hurt. There are some exceptions to this rule that will be governed by Karma. Don't worry about this, leave all matters out of your control to the universe to deal with.

The next step in this process now you have a list and have found the treasure is to accept all of it. It happened. It was supposed to. You are growing.

BE GRATEFUL FOR THE GOOD, BAD AND UGLY.

There is no end or beginning. Everything is one, constantly expanding and moving through time and space. What is light is dark, what is right is wrong, what is good is bad. Everything from a pure energy perspective has opposite poles which we learn to navigate to come into full soul consciousness.

Choose something that you need to forgive.

READ THIS, AND THEN DO THIS VISUALISATION.

Close your eyes.

Bring into your mind whatever it is you need to let go of...

Now sit in it, feel it and own it. It happened, you now know why. There was higher authority in this planning and that's ok with you. Imagine the thought at the top of a circle inside you. As you reflect and breathe, allow this thought to sink into a lighter circle, down, down, down to the bottom until you have reached a place of forgiveness.

Well done. Breathe...

Now, have a quick look at what this thought was again. Does it feel lighter than before?

GREAT

Leave that thought, now clean, kindly to the side and work through your whole list until everything has been cleaned and fully accepted as part of you, of your journey. What an incredible life you have had and how much growth has been achieved.

THE NEXT STEP IS SURRENDER. WE HAVE TO LET IT GO...

You will now have a pile of cleaned thoughts which are ready to go.

A process I developed as part of my journey was I sat in meditation on a mountain in Ibiza. I imagined this whole pile of cleaned thoughts sitting inside me waiting to be released. I imagined a beautiful Venetian glass box lined with pink velvet. I lifted the lid exhaling physically every drop of breath into the box with the remnants of my pain now cleaned, and shut the lid.

I said, "I am sorry, please forgive me, thank you, I love you, 11 times and with my mind I opened the box and let a million coloured butterflies drift up into the sky, further and further until I could no longer see them. I had released everything that no longer served me but I sat in appreciation for the huge amount of effort the universe had expended, orchestrating such a complex and perfectly laid out plan.

I felt physically lighter, joyous in fact. The pain was gone.

The only thing that will get in your way during this process is ego.

The mind wants us to stay trapped. Forgiveness is not who the mind is. Make sure you stay very present during this process so the mind cannot get involved. Be vigilant and kind. Ego is part of us, love this too. We just don't need it right at this moment!

YOU ARE THE MASTER.

The beauty of the Ho'oponopono system is that you can use it in everyday life. Let's say someone cuts you up in traffic. You forget your newfound composure and let rip. Bleep! Bleep! Bleep! Now you are engaged, ego is fired up, ready for battle. Now the mind is in control and starts to get busy.

Have I been caught on camera?

What if he follows me home?

Was I going too fast?

You are now going to worry about this for the whole day.

What a waste of energy. Whenever you snap and do something you wish you hadn't, forgive yourself straight away. It's like using an eraser on a blackboard.

Remove.

"I'm sorry, please forgive me, thank you, I love you" and it's done. Back to happy and positive thoughts and feelings.

Try not to feed the mind at all but if you do, you have a process to reverse this.

If you picture being in the mud every time you feel bad, jump back on the bridge and breathe. Focus towards the light, feel peaceful and start again. It's a process and we are only human after all. Forgive, forgive, and forgive.

WHAT A BEAUTIFUL WORLD WE ARE ENTERING.

Enjoy this process. Look at it as a stage where you will discover so much about WHY.

6

STAY OUT OF THE MUD

I trust you are beginning to feel whole. We will now start reprogramming you with positive habits.

I came across a wonderful book called, "The Five Agreements". The tools that are taught by Miguel Ruiz as the new keeper of this ancient knowledge preserved by the Nagual Masters of many centuries ago, helps you just become a better human. These tools also help you stay out of the mud!

THE FIRST AGREEMENT IS BEING IMPECCABLE WITH YOUR WORD.

The word is such an important tool in our toolbox. We can cause pain or love by the words we speak. Every letter of our language has a vibration, a frequency. When we spit poison at others, we literally poison them with toxic energy. Even thoughts can transfer this toxic energy.

If you have nothing nice to say, don't say anything at all.

Using your energy field to protect yourself, which you will learn in the next chapter, is a great way to ward off negativity, but if you are the one spitting poison, try saying these things back to yourself. You may need to hear them!

Gossiping plays a big factor here. Don't do it. The mind gets involved. You sit worrying about whether what you shared may be shared again, and you are back in the mind. Knowing that everything is energy, why would we want to pollute our world, yourself or others with toxic poison?

If you can master this one step, the others are easier as they are connected.

THE SECOND AGREEMENT IS DON'T MAKE ASSUMPTIONS.

We can never know what others are thinking. It's impossible. It depends totally on their state of mind and events happening in their life. Don't assume.

ASK.

So let's say you have just met a new man. You are excited to chat and he has planned to call you at 6pm.

6.30pm comes. No call. "WHY?" Perhaps he is out with guys from work?

Then at 8.30pm, "I bet he's had loads of drinks and is chatting up girls, what a cheek, we had a plan!"

11.00pm comes by at which point you have talked yourself out of liking him. You block him and that's it, over! He tries to call in the morning to let you know he was kept late at work and by the time he had finished it was fairly late and he didn't want to disturb you, but now he finds himself unable to make contact?

What a waste of what could have been.

Don't assume. You can never know what someone else is thinking unless you are a highly skilled clairvoyant and even then it's not constant. Don't blow what was intended!

THE THIRD AGREEMENT IS DON'T TAKE THINGS PERSONALLY.

When ego is predominant, any criticism is going to be met with opposition. NO I'm not! Your ego will defend your honour at any cost, but if you have prepared yourself to be protected from poison, you should be able to remove yourself fully from that attack to a place of centred calmness and contentment.

STICKS AND STONES!

Like all the tools I'm teaching you, this takes some work but if you are firmly rooted in the moment this step will be easy, ego will have subsided.

It's so exhausting dealing with people that you have to walk on egg shells with. You know whatever you say is going to be taken the wrong way. If this is the case, it may be time to relook at this relationship.

It's not worth the energy.

You may find you are beginning to see others in a new way and it is natural to change friends as you evolve. Just be kind and remove yourself gently. At the core of who we all are is pure love, but some still have to walk this path to remember who they are and behave accordingly.

THE FOURTH AGREEMENT IS ALWAYS DO YOUR BEST.

Discovering purpose greatly helps with this step. It's much easier to do your best at what you love, but you can apply this to every area of your life.

Doing your best gives you a sense of satisfaction. Thin down your tasks if you are feeling overwhelmed, do what you enjoy and your vibration stays high helping encourage good things into your life. "The joy is in the journey."

THE FIFTH AGREEMENT IS BE SCEPTICAL BUT LEARN TO LISTEN.

In a day and age where scams are commonplace, and will be more so, a good rule of thumb is if it seems too good to be true it probably is. Someone who listens is by far wiser. Take note when you are out. Who is at the centre puffing their feathers grandly while captivating the audience? What did they learn during that evening? Nothing. And what did you learn, loads!

Being a good listener is a great skill to learn. Knowledge is power.

I can't begin to tell you how important these agreements are. They keep you out of the mud. They keep you sane. Integrate these into your daily life and see how quickly things change.

7

SUPERPOWERS

We have superpowers that we have forgotten how to use. We are conscious creators on the leading edge of thought and we have inbuilt warning and information centres which are there to guide us.

INTUITION, FOR EXAMPLE.

The solar plexus is the centre most commonly used to distinguish right from wrong but I tend to use my heart chakra more often as I get clearer signals in this location.

By staying present and focussing your attention on your physical heart, ask yourself the series of questions below and look out for any feelings of lifting, bubbles, heat or a skip in beat, anything unusual.

If I feel a lift, I know it's a yes. If nothing, it's a no. If it's a really bad no, I get a knot in my stomach. "Trust your gut" is a saying that explains this perfectly. The more you do this, the stronger this muscle becomes and is therefore easier to read.

Imagine having internal radar that is connected to all knowledge of the universe to guide you.

I'M HAPPY TO TELL YOU, YOU DO!

Read this, and then practise this visualisation.

Close your eyes.

Bring your attention to your heart centre. Become your heart, feel it beat, feel the blood flowing through your veins, feel the power and precise function of this organ, and become it.

Now ask yourself some questions and watch out for movement.

Am I (insert name)

Am I a being of eternal light?

Do I love myself?

Do I love my family?

Could I do better?

Am I on track for where I need to be?

Am I loved?

What did you feel?

The more you practise this, the more you will TRUST the process.

Another superpower we have is our energy field. We can increase this to provide protection if needed.

Read this, and then practise this visualisation.

Close your eyes.

Bring your focus to heart centre. Be aware of tingly energy throughout your body. The more you focus on this, the more you can force this to expand.

Use your mind. Notice how the energy field around you is about 40cm away from your body. Feel your skin under the weight of the energy field.

Now with your mind, push your energy out to the edges of the room. Feel how small you feel, how protected you are by your own force.

Allow this to come back to normal and open your eyes.

You can use this when you feel vulnerable. Other people can feel your energy even though they can't see it or know of its existence in most cases.

Another great use for this technique is when someone is spitting poison at you, which you learnt in the last chapter. Protect yourself, you have the power.

Trust is the ultimate goal, trust in self, trust in universal knowledge and orchestration. Trust the creative process.

THE NEXT LEVEL OF LEARNING HAS TO BE ABOUT JUDGEMENT.

As a society we are used to opposites, good and bad, right and wrong, left and right. These are the options we feel comfortable with, the linear perception of life, but when we adopt a higher perspective things change and what was important no longer is.

Nothing good has ever come of using this archaic system of fear and control. There is always a loser and a winner.

I came across an ancient yoga philosophy during my journey, VIVEKA.

This offers a wonderful alternative.

This philosophy is based on what is eternal and what is not.

Try turning your hands to top and bottom rather than from side to side to grasp this.

The top is eternal. Does what you are judging comply to universal completeness and expansion from a place of pure love or does it comply with non eternal which means it's temporary and of no consequence?

Let me give you a couple of examples.

Lets say you are criticising what someone is wearing or that the table you ordered came in the wrong shade. Both of these would be non eternal. They have no part to play in the higher picture. They are things and therefore have no importance in our attention.

Let's say, like me, I have chosen a career that helps contribute to a global rising of our planet which will greatly affect the universe and everything in it. This would be eternal and therefore should be pursued.

Loving someone and looking after them would be eternal as you are behaving as your authentic self.

What this shows you here is that everything that is non eternal is of no importance. Question everything. Only concentrate on matters eternal that make you feel good universally and are for the greater good of man.

Get out and stay out of the mud. There are more important things to be doing.

BEING HAPPY FOR ONE!

When we start putting all of these pieces together, we start seeing things very differently. We see Truth. You have just had a glimpse from the top step, the doorway to enlightenment.

YOU GET OUT WHAT YOU PUT IN.

Use the time before the next lesson to practise using your powers and looking at things from a much more detached perspective, as an observer, and see the underlying truth that was there but not visible before.

8

IT'S ALL ABOUT VIBRATION

How is life looking now?

Are you beginning to see that perhaps what you thought was reality is actually an illusion? The only thing we need to concern ourselves with is being happy, using our gifts to help humanity and behaving like a good human. If we can make enough money by doing what we love, pay the bills and have a little over for extras, this is considered a great life.

When you sit in TRUST, the mind becomes free. You know that whatever comes into your life is through thought which will become your reality.

Let me give you an example.

One person is happy and sits in trust. They see everything as it actually is, comprehensive and stunningly beautiful. They exist in the NOW and don't worry about HOW or WHEN but instinctively know ALL will come.

The person above will see beauty in all; will sit in flow and trust. They will see signs everywhere of opportunities and love. They will attract the vibration of happiness and the universe will expand accordingly, delivering what they desire.

The second person is anxious and depressed, consumed with worry about the future and regret from the past. Everything looks gloomy, desperate and hopeless.

This person's life is gloomy. The vibration of worry, regret and pain will be coming back in bounds.

Nothing will change until action is taken to control the mind.

The interesting thing is these two people can be in the same location, the same family even, the same level of wealth and network, but one has found the secret, the other not.

From my own personal experience, I can tell you this is fact. The two years I sat in "Poor Me" I attracted everything I didn't want, no work, no money, no friends, no love, no food in the fridge, no confidence etc.

I even had cockroaches and mice. I really must have been emitting a low vibration! When I started doing this work, things changed, opportunities started appearing, and my visualisation board began delivering results.

Things began to change.

All I can say is if you are skim reading this before you start the work, if your life is not good, do the work. It's worth every moment.

So, we have got to the stage in this process where we can now start looking at the Law of Attraction. How does it work and does it work?

There are a lot of myths out there about this subject. I would say it definitely works, but not perhaps in the way you think.

If you are starting to feel comfortable that we are energy beings and the whole universe is energy, then it may be feasible to imagine that creation can be

born by thought alone. Thought creates a frequency and when that frequency is matched it is law that manifestation will occur.

If you do not yet follow Esther Hicks who channels Abraham, an entity of spirit that educates the world about this very topic, I highly recommend you do. Esther has hundreds of videos on YouTube. If you are feeling flat, listen to one of her recordings, especially at bedtime, it will lift you.

Another point to bring up here is that the vibration you go to sleep with is the one you wake up with, so ensure your vibration is high at night. Practise gratitude, spend some time connecting with your inner self, send love to others in thought, and sit in contentment and trust.

When you wake up in the morning, you will already be almost ready for a great day. So, after a quick meditation, affirmations and a calm start, your day can be nothing short of wonderful. You have learnt many tools now to keep you balanced, so use them and make them part of your everyday life.

So the process is...

1.   ASK
2.   THE UNIVERSE STARTS ORCHESTRATING
3.   BE OPEN TO RECEIVE

The first two steps are easy. We are constantly throwing our desires out to the universe in forms of wishes, prayers or requests. The universe then starts immediate work putting all the parts together for you and then if you are sitting in present contentment and trust you will start seeing steps delivered to you that will help you achieve whatever it is you wished for.

I will give you an example of how quickly this can work when you stay in high vibration.

I had a few things I was thinking about for my day. I needed a celebrity to help me get the message out about what I was doing. I also needed a plumber and a roofer for a project I was helping a friend with. My energy was good...

I was feeling grateful for a beautiful sunny day and happy to be alive.

As I walked from my office to meet a surveyor 5 minutes away, I bumped into a local premier footballer who I spent half an hour discussing this project with. I then saw a plumber's van drive past with a lovely smiley guy so I photographed his signage and two minutes later a roofer passed in a van and again gave me a wonderful smile. I photographed his number too and made contact with them both. They both did a wonderful job on the project.

Thank you universe.

This shows how quickly manifestation can occur. They were not life changing things but they were what I was asking for through thought.

There are so many other stories about manifestation that I can share but by now you should be in a position to start seeing this for yourself.

Get your vibration high, stay in the moment, trust everything will appear and don't worry about the how or when. The universe is a million steps ahead of you and knows exactly what you need and when you need it. If what you're asking for is not for your highest good, better alternatives will appear.

You don't need to focus all day on what you desire, this will create anxiety. Just focus on feeling good and enjoy life. The rest will unfold.

You can create a visualisation board to strengthen the energy towards your desires. Cut out anything that represents what you want and put onto a board and hang this somewhere you can see often. You can also make a desire box that you open in a year. Just fold up any ideas, pictures, clippings of anything you desire and put it into the box. In a year's time, empty the box and see what has appeared in your life. It's quiet remarkable what you see arrive.

THE WHOLE SECRET TO MANIFESTING IS ABOUT YOUR VIBRATION.

Another tip if you stray off the feeling of contentment is to focus straight away on the breath. Focus, focus, focus, regardless of what you're doing. The air filling your body is your life blood, this encourages gratitude. This focus brings you back into the moment, centre, and out of the mind. Take some time to bring yourself back into balance, feel it and when you are ready you can continue again being joyous.

It takes time to master always being in balance, but it does come so keep with it. Nothing worth having ever comes easily but easily is delivered in return!

Enjoy the process and have fun with this. Look out for thoughts of inspiration, often the steps delivered are in the form of a great idea. If it makes you feel excited and motivated, this is a thought worth developing. Use your intuition as you have learnt and stay gratefully alert.

Magic does happen.

THE NEW WORLD

Lesson Nine and Ten in my ON DEMAND and one to one programme focuses on the soul's journey, soul ages and our spiritual DNA. Why we are like we are.

My intention for this book was to simplify my teaching to be more accessible to people of any faith or belief. If you want to explore higher knowing, I would highly recommend doing my ON DEMAND programme. There are many visualisations, meditations and a deeper study of all the subjects we have covered here. It's difficult to articulate everything in writing but I hope I have given you some inspiration, hope and guidance of how to live a happy and fulfilled life.

If you follow all of these steps and do any additional learning that appears during this process and use the tools I teach you, life will never look the same again. You will find equanimity, peace, love and joy.

You are an extraordinary being of light. You have powers beyond anything you imagined and life can be delicious if you commit to finding self and doing some inner work to raise your consciousness. WE ARE WE. Everything is connected including all humans. Remember this on your journey. Show kindness and compassion for one another and our beautiful planet that we have been gifted to enjoy. We don't own it. We are visitors, guests. Behave accordingly so our stay is aligned.

Each and every one of us is here to design and participate in a perfect world and to experience a magnificent life but we all need to do the work to WAKE UP.

WHAT WILL THE NEW WORLD LOOK LIKE?

Well, this depends on us. Collectively we are all in charge of how the new world is to be formed and experienced. It is my gut feeling that this awakening is going to take time and I do believe Mother Nature will hold the reins and manage this until we are ready. We touched briefly on pain being the biggest motivator. Humans are extremely stubborn and often need a little push, or in my case, a huge push!

It all begins with asking yourself,

Who Am I?

No inner journey can commence without being ready to discover the answer to this fundamental question. I welcome you and support you on this amazing journey. Life changing doesn't come close and what you will find is that the world you hoped for is already here, you just couldn't see it!

HISTORY IN THE MAKING

We are currently entering week 4 in the corona virus lockdown in London.

There have been 1,981,239 confirmed cases of COVID 19. 486,662 have recovered and there have been 126,681 deaths. In the UK, there seems to be a slight slow down due to social distancing. A gentle integration of some services is being discussed but I feel we have many more weeks/months before any kind of normality will be restored.

Then there is the question of a second wave expected in Oct/Nov 2020. My gut is telling me there will also be natural events of cleansing to come next, perhaps a tsunami or volcanic eruption. We will have to bide our time patiently and see how this unfolds.

I knew this time was coming two years ago. I wasn't sure of the shape it would take but I did know we were to move to a higher dimension, so

I trust my gut in knowing everything will be perfect and to be open to all possible future events.

MY SPIRITS ARE HIGH.

The secret to this is that I have done the work. I can instantly feel when the mind tries to dominate my experience and I can take appropriate steps to come back into balance quickly. Ego will always be part of who we are, but the more work you do, the further you can move from this to experience a more empowered and happy life.

Keeping busy with creative activities helps you connect to higher consciousness. Our DNA is going through a natural upgrade as we sleep. The more light and happiness we can experience, the faster this upgrade will happen and the more delicious life will become.

The more you awaken, the more you see, and that includes old patterns of fear still being lived out by many. Complaining, blaming and living in scarcity are all tell-tale signs of the old way. Where are you currently?

We have all chosen this lifetime. In fact we fought to be here at this incredible time to see and be part of what is happening right now. We all have a part to play in this.

THIS IS HISTORY IN THE MAKING.

I'm not sure what is the biggest fear being experienced by the world currently. Is it being out of control? Is it of dying? Is it of the unknown? Probably a mixture of these. Let's break this down to understand more.

BEING OUT OF CONTROL.

The structure of the old world was always about control and manipulation. The rich use control and use this to govern the less well off. Media has had a good run of keeping us trapped in fear. You very rarely see a feel good story. It's always negative and leaves you feeling anxious.

Try and remove yourself from the news till you are stronger.

My feeling is the future will see more positive media content, celebrating the innovate nature of the human race rather than what is wrong with it. Again, we will have to see how this takes shape, but I do anticipate big change ahead.

FEAR OF DYING.

We touched on this briefly in chapter two. Our ego is there to prevent us from dying so whilst you remain governed by ego, you will live in fear.

What do you actually have to fear?

This might not be the belief of everyone reading this, but my understanding and belief is that we are energy beings, all connected and part of source, god or whatever you like to call "creation." If we are energy, this is eternal.

Energy is forever expanding and cannot be affected by any amount of pain experienced in our lifetimes which is to provide growth. Our current lifetimes are part of many grand cycles. This equates to thousands of lifetimes, not only on earth but on other planets and dimensions, so what do we have to fear?

Life, in the here and now is just a temporary experience of which there have been many before and many more to come.

THE JOY IS IN THE JOURNEY.

I have no fear of dying. I see life as a continuous cycle. I'm excited to one day be able to return "home" or to "full knowing", to plan another experience and to return again to carry out what is needed next time for me to progress.

When you look at life like this, fear no longer governs you. You are happy to go with the flow and live every day as it comes in the moment.

If you choose to end this temporary life at this time, you will have to return at the same growth level next time and face similar challenges, so my advice is, learn the tools I outline and find a way through this.

Trust all will be well and it will be, perhaps not in the way you were once used to, but relevant to your new perception.

As a guide, we live about 200 physical lifetimes as part of one grand cycle. The number of cycles range from approximately 4 to 19. I am almost at the end of my 11th cycle. I am an old soul level 5 and have a few more lifetimes to complete in this cycle before I can start the upper journey back to source to start another grand cycle on another planet or dimension in the future. It is possible for me to complete this cycle in this lifetime, depending on how much is achieved. I have 22/4 in the position of spiritual goal in my

Soul Plan which means final completion and accomplishment. This drives me forward.

It's good to remember that the soul is not in a rush. We have free will to do as we wish. We are always in control and supported at soul level. We are loved.

FEAR OF THE UNKNOWN.

If you knew what was to come, how would that affect how you live?

There wouldn't be much point. There would be nothing to aim for, to grow from, no excitement or wonder. Humans like drama. We like to be challenged, we like to achieve, so there can be no other way than taking baby steps and staying present as the journey unfolds. Intuition becomes stronger the more work you do and this helps guide you.

So next time you are feeling anxious about the unknown, turn your perspective into excitement about what is to come while remaining in the present moment. This not only helps you escape the mind but it raises your vibration encouraging manifestation and helps you experience life in gratitude.

TURN YOUR BELIEFS AROUND AND SEE HOW YOUR LIFE CHANGES!

Can you imagine how beautiful our world would be if everyone practised everything you have learnt so far? How life would play out if everyone supported each other and lived life as a precious gift rather than the expected struggle that has been spoon fed to us to accept since birth.

Now that is a day to look forward to and it is coming. You can play your part in this. As you rise, you influence others. The vibration of the planet lifts and we will exist in a state of higher consciousness and bliss. We all have a choice!

I can already see how things are beginning to change.

Appreciation for our health and key workers

Neighbours looking out for each other

9000 volunteers signed up to help the NHS

Government becoming more social and accountable

The flood of good feeling on social media supporting those in isolation

Talk is cheap. Action is what is needed at this time.

We can learn from past events to see how quickly we tend to go back to old ways. The tsunami that hit South East Asia in 2004 created an overwhelming global vibration of compassion. This was short lived and quickly forgotten as it didn't affect everyone. This current pandemic is affecting every person on the planet and I trust will be significant enough to bring about wonderful change for us all.

We are all in this together and I don't mean just coping. I mean connectivity, love, compassion and peace. We have spent centuries praying, meditating, asking for a world of peace and love. Well, here is the opportunity. We have received exactly what we have been asking for, an opportunity to change.

Ask and it is given, always...

SYNCHRONICITY

The number 11 has great significance. In numerology, it represents double creativity and confidence, brings intuition and spiritual insight, sensitivity and empathy which holds enormous power both mentally and physically.

We have learnt in chapter four the significance of understanding numerology. Numbers are the foundations of everything that exists.

Numerology is being looked at more closely by scientists and philosophers in this age to try and unlock ancient secrets and learning.

Much is still to be uncovered.

11/2, 22/4 AND 33/6 ARE ALL MASTER NUMBERS IN NUMEROLOGY.

As I mentioned before, I am a 22/4, Master Builder. This is only a small part of who I am but is significant in the choices I have made during this lifetime.

I love to build things!

The two 2s represent cooperation and balance. When you have a double number, the challenges you have chosen will be more difficult. The first 2 is inner cooperation and balance, the second 2 is outer cooperation and balance. This has resulted in overgiving and retracting most of my life but I do feel now I have mastered these to the degree that I can start focussing on the life path number, which in my case is 4, process and stability. Baby steps!

To find out why you behave the way you do is eye opening. It explains so much about your inner being. We are extremely complex creatures.

As a line of reassurance, your soul would never choose a set of circumstances that you couldn't handle in this lifetime, so if you are stuck, or lost, do the work to understand who you are. It helps you see patterns of the past and helps you break down walls in the future.

Interestingly, I have taught more 33/6 Master Teachers than any other number. I have been sent teachers to help them step into their roles, to allow them to bring their gifts into the world.

With eyes wide open, I love seeing how everything stiches together. It is fascinating and really helps you become more in tune with who you really are.

Once you start seeing the bigger picture, you start remembering. The veil is lifted and you step into who you authentically are.

This is our primary work on earth, to remember who we are.

12

MIDLIFE CRISIS

We touched briefly in the opening preface about how my journey started.

It is often through loss or grief or midlife crisis that we are encouraged to make change. In my case stubbornness was key to this process. I sat in pain for almost two years sinking deeper and deeper into despair. I no longer wanted to be here. I had lost everything, to the tune of about £11million.

You can imagine the shock of once being able to do anything I wanted at any time, to being trapped, hungry, depressed and without hope. It was a huge shock to my system on top of not being able to look after my daughter anymore while still reeling from a recent divorce was the straw that broke the camels back. This affected my mental, physical and emotional body. I couldn't have experienced much more. There wasn't much else that could happen!

Everyone's awakening is different. There are no hard fast rules. I documented my entire journey through this difficult period which enabled me to go back and review all the steps I had taken and design and build the WHO AM I programme.

I learnt everything in the wrong order. I stumbled across books, teachers and courses that helped me grow, but it wasn't until I got close to five years of study that I started to see how it all works.

My journey spans almost a decade. I have invested time and energy in identifying the secrets to finding authentic happiness. I couldn't do what I do now without having done this work. Not only have I been there, but also I have found the way out and now teach this to others. It's kind of beautiful really that something so painful could result in something so uplifting and beautiful. When you look at this in perspective, you see that everything happens for a reason.

My fundamental energies are as a creator and a teacher. Healing is not dominant in my energy, but what I teach heals. Education not medication is the answer and is available to everyone who is prepared to put in the work.

The beauty of what I do is I shortcut the process for clients by about 5 years. This truly is a gift for anyone who wants to escape hard times quickly.

I have revised and amended my programme several times over the last three years. I invested my first year in helping pro bono clients. I had never been a teacher before. I had to step into this role gradually. Through this process, I was able to find my feet without feeling nervous as what I was doing was from a place of pure kindness and was greatly appreciated by the people I was helping. It takes time to build a business especially when you change direction.

My programme was revised and amended a second time before taking on paid clients. This version served me until the end of 2019 when I adapted my programme for online lessons to be available ON DEMAND. There seemed to be a degree of urgency about filming these lessons. All the pieces I needed fell into place very easily. I raised a little investment, found a brilliant videographer, learnt how to create a hosting platform and created a new website. All of this was completed just before Christmas of 2019, just in time to be able to help now.

Synchronicity? Definitely!

I have taught over 100 private clients since I began my practice, people from all walks of life, from CEO to teacher, from film makers to financial analysts, from housewives to celebrities. If it is part of your life plan to be depressed to allow you to awaken, it will happen. If you have made an agreement for me to help you, you will find me.

I have learnt so much from teaching. Questions arise during sessions so additional learning has been achieved in real time. I am now an accomplished Master and am excited about how this will unfold over the coming years.

THIS IS MY TIME. I WAS BORN TO DO THIS.

I am in no rush. I am enjoying the process. The joy is in the journey. Everything is unfolding in its own perfect time, and the beauty is, I have so many awakened souls around me now assisting me from a higher place of consciousness. I thank you if you are one of these beautiful souls that have already crossed my path helping me evolve thus far.

My goal is to help heal the world. I trust with many versions of my teaching now available, will help as many people as possible.

SO WHAT DOES "AWAKE" FEEL LIKE?

It's hard to imagine from a place of "ASLEEP". It is not until you "WAKEUP" that you feel this, but let me try and articulate this for you.

You will feel excitement and anticipation for what is yet to come.

You will be in control of the mind and exist in positivity and grace.

You will push yourself to experience every drop of NOWNESS as this is what makes your heart expand with joy.

You will feel connectivity, inspiration, oneness, and gratitude seeing the beauty in all.

You will manifest from thought.

You will know exactly who you are and understand your challenges better.

You will have a newfound empathy for others.

You will no longer be driven from a place of lack, scarcity or fear.

Money will no longer be your primary focus.

Helping others will be your predominant direction.

You will think from a higher perspective, almost like being an observer.

You will exist in equanimity and experience a calm composure not usually felt.

You will feel empowered, light and clear in knowing.

You will sit in trust, you will not judge, gossip or cause pain to others.

You will operate from a newfound integrity. You will become authentic.

You will experience joy and bliss in every moment.

You will know exactly who you are, why you are here and what you are here to do.

Now if that list doesn't inspire you to take action, I can't imagine what will!

If you're feeling sad or anxious, it is better to take action as soon as possible. It gets harder the more you travel down the negative spiral of despair.

But you are in charge and when it's time, you will know.

10 weeks to change your life?

For me, it's a no brainer.

LIFE CYCLES

Unlucky for some!

I never look at numbers in the way they are written. I see numbers as signs. Door numbers, car number plates, signs that appear every day on your phone, phone numbers etc. are all signs that can be read.

You can tell the nature of a household by the number of the house.   Imagine having this insight!

Another fascinating element to numbers is that the year we are in also determines the flavour of what is to be experienced.

For example, 2020 is a 4 year in a 9 year cycle.

2+0+2+0 = 4

2020 is about process and stability, setting firm roots so our lofty castles don't fall over!   This energy is very much the underlying force behind what is happening right now. We are finding new stability through process.

Next year, 2021 for example is about freedom and discipline. We will have established firm roots from going through the awakening process this year. We will be released from fear and will have new found discipline.

The blooms will appear next spring. Be ready to see them.

Every 9 years we go into a new cycle. To know when is the right time to start a business, find love or to sit quietly will greatly help you in the planning of your life.

The financial crash for example happened in a 9 year, 2007, 2+0+0+7 = 9. This was the end of a cycle, a closing ready for new birth in 2008, 2+0+0+8= 10 (you do not use the 0 in calculations). This was a 1 year, creativity and higher knowing, new beginnings.

A really beautiful exercise to do is map a list of years from now back to when you were born. Split them into 9 year cycles and add life events that happened in that corresponding year. See a pattern emerge. All years total what part of the cycle we are in.

IF YOU IMAGINE THE CYCLE TO BE AS FOLLOWS:

YEAR ONE

Dark, hard, no visible growth, seeds are planted but need nurturing.

YEAR TWO

Roots start to sprout, you are beginning to make headway but only tiny shoots are visible. Hope is gained from seeing new growth.

YEAR THREE

Stronger roots and shoots appear. The waiting has been worthwhile and things are beginning to appear. We start finding our voice.

YEAR FOUR

Buds are beginning to appear, steps need to be reviewed and completed to provide structure to your life.

YEAR FIVE

Flowers open, a certain freedom is felt. The fruit of your labour is beginning to appear.

YEAR SIX

Seeds begin to disperse, to reseed, to give back, and to provide abundance.

YEAR SEVEN

Petals start to fall and introspection begins. Bring in the harvest. How did you do? What can be learnt? How can you give back?

YEAR EIGHT

Everything starts going back to earth. Energy is being preserved and reflection is necessary. You learn to sit in trust.

YEAR NINE

Back to the soil, rest, regroup, reflection, harvest, just BE.

If you follow this as a guide whatever your endeavours, it shows when you can expect what is coming and align this energy to your plans.

For example, I started WHO AM I in a year one. I'm absolutely in line with universal flow. I am in balance. I know where I am and when things will appear. This takes all the angst out of guessing.

So in this regard, next year for me is the year I will start seeing the fruits of my labour. I know it, so I believe it, so it will be.

That's just how it works.

REMOVE THE GUESSWORK AND GET MORE IN LINE WITH UNIVERSAL ENERGIES AND FLOW.

THE NEW WORLD

Collaboration and partnerships are key to all businesses and relationships especially as we enter the new world. Having the support and additional skills sets you don't personally possess, will be key to the rebuilding.

My aim is to join forces with mental health providers and the NHS eventually, to lead the way in how mental health is managed. This will take time as alternative medicine is still not trusted. The old way is heavily reliant on using drugs, but this only keeps you "ASLEEP", numb and detached from growth, not to mention the damage this is doing to our world.

Our food chain is toxic, our water contaminated, our ozone depleted to a wafer thin layer which is the difference between being able to exist in a climatically controlled environment or being fried by the sun.

We are already seeing a cleaner atmosphere, cleaner rivers. Animals are enjoying a quieter world, and the world is coming back into balance. If this can be achieved in a matter of months, can you imagine how quickly we could reverse this damage to our beautiful world?

The one thing I know for sure is life will never return to the way it was. How different it will be, depends on each and every one of us. We are all responsible for this world while we are here and when and if you come round to the idea of reincarnation, the world we create today is not only for future generations, it's for us to return to...

Perhaps this understanding will help deliver a better world?

The planet doesn't need us as I said before. We need it as our temporary home to carry out our life journeys. Be mindful of this. Think before taking actions. Every tiny change by each of us, adds up to great change by the collective. We can do this.

HOW WILL BUSINESS LOOK IN THE FUTURE?

Very differently!

We are already seeing key players going into liquidation. Many businesses that support the old way will struggle to find traction in the new world. As people awaken, they will be less inclined to buy stuff which we know from past experience doesn't make us happy. This will reduce deliveries, air pollution, spending and landfill.

I do see more and more people growing fruit and veg at home. Many people have huge gardens and these should be utilised to reduce air miles of food being flown in from the four corners of the globe to support a more local, healthy and affordable diet. Many children especially in urban cities have no idea how to grow food, where certain foods come from or how diet affects our wellbeing. We all need to become more responsible and less lazy.

Osteopaths will be needed to deal with damaged posture and spinal injuries due to a decade of mobile phone screen gazing.

Counsellors and therapists will be in high demand. In my opinion, it is necessary that therapists update their methods to adapt to bringing people into the present moment and teach rather than just listening to trauma and pain.

Talking about the past keeps you trapped there.

I see governments handing more over to local communities to manage. I see local residents becoming more involved in duties within communities as services are already overstretched and flailing, and we will have to do more.

This won't go down well with those still ASLEEP which is why it is so vital for everyone to wake up if possible.

Much is to be done to rebuild our world and take it gracefully into the 22nd century.

What we do is what we will receive.

THIS IS A LOVELY IDEA BUT I CAN'T SEE THIS HAPPENING JUST YET.

Offices that are now empty due to the lockdown could be reused as low cost housing to support key workers and lower paid workers in high density cities. Business cities could be built on the outskirts instead offering flexi working conditions for employees to cut down on travel costs, emissions and congestion. This would greatly reduce overheads for businesses and provide thriving inclusive work communities in areas that could easily support these.

At the end of the day, it's only ego that says, "Look at me, I'm based in London W1." Ego has much to answer for. Once tamed, everything changes.

The media moguls will loose control of the common man, as man will be able to see beyond the fear-based propaganda currently being fed. More responsible and supportive reporting will need to be introduced to encourage the newly awakened to remain engaged. Being a journalist will become more enjoyable!

I see "look at me" social media trailing off. So many people see how damaging it is to be constantly bombarded with noise. When there is no one to impress, the bikini dancers will get bored and perhaps new social interaction will be formed based more on honest need and supply, creating an environment of support and legacy rather than hard selling. You could achieve the same results if everyone swapped services, especially in the beginning stages of our new world. Everything is going to be extremely tight and we will need an alternative way of existing for many years to come following this pandemic.

I see the mega rich learning to unburden themselves by compassionate giving. So many are already adopting this. If we are to become a nation of oneness, the division between poor and rich will have to be resolved.

No one person is better than another. We have just chosen a different life plan this time around. Being rich is just as heavy a burden as being poor. They both give us the capacity for great learning and action.

WE ARE NOT WHAT WE HAVE!

So the new world will look very different. Many jobs will be lost but new opportunities will arise. It will take time. Perhaps I'm being overly optimistic but being a visionary I am always 10 years ahead of the market. The new world will be remarkable, once we get there.

I am excited about what is to come. Any change will help shift these stale and non-serving energies. Will there be opposition to the new world? Oh yes! Will these few become obsolete? Yes, definitely. People will have a choice. Adapt or sink.

There is a saying that has always stuck with me. I'm not at all religious but there seemed to be an element of meaning to this that rang true...

THE MEEK SHALL INHERIT THE EARTH.

The other scenario that could happen is that all those leaving earth currently are chosen for a new world as discussed widely by Dolores Cannon.

She talks about a new world being formed in a new dimension. If you haven't read the convoluted universe series, I highly recommend this set of 6 books. They open your mind to many other possibilities.

In book two, Dolores talks about Gaia energy leaving earth. Those ready will go to the new world and those that remain will fight it out till maximum growth is achieved at this level. Once all life form is gone from planet earth, the process of repair will begin over millions of years to allow return or reseeding in the future. I would be most intrigued to know the predominant beliefs of people that have passed during this pandemic. Is there a common thread? Are they the ones who deserve the new world now?

Are they the meek?

All will become clear over time. We just have to be patient.

CHILDREN OF THE STARS

We are children of the stars, created in the eternal furnace of space, all part of the same energy that was cast out into the universe 13.7 billion years ago.

Some sparks of energy became planets, galaxies, living creatures, matter but we are all part of the same 92 chemical compounds that make up the universe as we know it.

We can see far out into space. We can use light being bounced back to recognise the chemical makeup of other planets. The colour that is radiated back from planets can be deciphered very accurately to show exact chemical compounds to be found on each planet. If you haven't yet discovered Professor Brian Cox, I highly recommend, "The Wonders of the Universe" series. This explains this in great detail.

In our Milky Way alone, there are more planets in this one galaxy than there are grains of sand on all the beaches on our planet, and there are billions of galaxies just like the Milky Way. This starts to put into perspective the enormity of what is around us.

We know the universe is constantly expanding, moving through space and time at thousands of miles per hour. Eventually Andromeda will engulf our Milky Way and create a new galaxy. Earth may or may not be swallowed into a black hole at this point, but the universe is constantly eating itself and creating new life. Everything is in constant motion. This isn't expected for another 4.5 billion years. I expect humans will be long gone by then.

So seeing the enormity of what is rather than what most see, a street, a neighbourhood a country and a planet, we must gaze in awe at the complexity of everything, knowing that what happens to one part influences all other parts.

WE ARE WE

Are we under scrutiny from other parts of the universe? My belief is if earth can support life, so can others. Will life be in a familiar context? Very unlikely. Creation adapts according to its surroundings.

With eyes wide open, anything is possible. The fine balance of life and all that this brings is likely to be more than we can ever imagine.

Humans are not superior, we are just a species that inhabits this planet, and to date, not what you would hope to find on another world.

What would your opinion of earth be if you were a visitor here?

It is very interesting to view top down. It gives you a very different view of what IS.

A beautiful exercise to do when you're feeling overwhelmed is put your conscious energy out into the universe and look at earth from there. Your problems will pale into insignificance as you see the orchestration of the bigger picture.

A GOOD LIFE IS NOT A LIFE WITHOUT PROBLEMS; A GOOD LIFE IS A LIFE WITH GOOD PROBLEMS.

OPPORTUNITIES EXIST EVERYWHERE.

16

THOUGHTS CREATE THINGS

As we have discussed in an earlier chapter, thoughts create things. With this in mind, visualising a world we wish to see when we come out on the other side of this pandemic makes perfect sense.

Collective thought creates substantial change. This has been proved many times in the past where mass meditation has created less crime, improved health and global wellbeing.

We are currently in week four of lockdown in the UK. Mental health problems are beginning to be felt by most. People are restless and anxious as no definite plan has been reached by government about when things may improve. People are focussing on the news and tying themselves into the problem which is feeding the ego, keeping them trapped.

I can feel the level of anxiety in the air. If I hadn't spent years training my mind and coming into full soul consciousness, to see from a higher perspective, I know I would also be feeling very nervous and stressed.

I can see that the level of trauma experienced during this time is going to have long lasting effects around the world.

Learning to master the mind is probably the most important thing we can learn to do. If we talk about and constantly view the problem, these will manifest into reality. A way of reversing this is to imagine your proffered reality.

READ THIS AND THEN DO THIS EXERCISE.

What does your proffered reality look like? Think about this for a moment.

Close your eyes.

Imagine you have a tunnel coming from your third eye, (at the centre of your forehead). Allow yourself to enter the tunnel and become really present. Notice the walls, the floors, the temperature. Notice how excited you are to be going to your special place. Be in this moment.

As you turn the bend, you will see a light. As you get closer, you can start seeing your special place. Step out into it and feel how happy you feel. Stay as long as you like; decorate it with your imagination. Use your five senses to fully experience this.

What does it look like? Where is it? Who is there? What can you smell? What is the temperature like? What sounds can you hear? What are you wearing?

Once you are ready to leave, go back to the edge of the tunnel and walk backwards until you turn the bend and feel the room behind you. Come back to where you are sitting or lying down

This is a wonderful technique if you are having problems sleeping. Stay in your proffered reality all night if you wish!

Besides stimulating right brain, which naturally makes you feel less stressed, it also tells the universe, "I want this." If everyone's visualisation portrayed bliss and happiness, free from restriction and pain and suffering, this is the world we would all live in. It can be no other way.

Like unto itself is drawn.

Have fun with this exercise. Include other people you want with you even though they may not be in your reality yet.

Be creative.

It is reported that when we are in higher planes between physical life times, we are able to teleport, telecommunicate, jump from one side of the universe to the other, simply using thought. We have superpowers but we have forgotten how to use them. The more we trust, believe and practice, the stronger our abilities become. Your reality changes and so does your perception.

The task ahead seems so enormous at this time but actually if each and every one of us on earth changed our perception, the world would be awake and oneness would prevail. What a day this will be!

LIFE IS WHAT YOU THINK.

If you have carried out the steps explained thus far, you will understand this chapter. If you haven't yet started, go back and undertake these as they are set out. My teaching is designed in steps. Each one needs to be done in the right order with as much attention as you can to start seeing things differently and when you do, you start feeling physically, spiritually and mentally better.

17

BE THAT

DISCOVER WHO YOU ARE AND BE THAT.

There is no better feeling than that of acceptance of who you are, to not worry about what others think. You become powerful and resilient.

You have learnt the steps to focus on your internal being rather than what you look like or have or have not in this world.

There are many other facets to our personality. If you want to delve deeper and do more self discovery, please do my ON DEMAND programme. Lessons 1, 9 and 10 are focussed on higher knowing, about your soul journey and spiritual DNA.

Remembering who you are is most commonly sought around midlife. This is the monad where reflection becomes predominant. You start to look back.

Did I do what I came to do?

Is this where I want to be going?

The ego and essence, if not manually trained in advance, come to a point of handover around midlife. The ego doesn't want to let go but the soul essence wants to assist in the golden years and onto death to help you experience a slightly different experience. This stage can be very traumatic especially if reflection shows you no longer want to do what you did. This is a scary time. I know. I went through this. I had no idea how I was going to start another business at the age of 50 with no capital.

But I did. The universe helped. I remained in trust. I stayed present and enjoyed the journey. If I can, you can. Baby steps. Make sure you have identified what makes you happy, how you can best serve humanity using your special gifts. Start very slowly to avoid feeling overwhelmed. In a few years, you will be established and doing what you love.

While in this building phase, feel how what you are building will feel like once you are in flow. Remain in contentment during this process. Do your best. Make sure you have studied your Soul Plan to make sure you understand your purpose and enjoy the journey. The more you are aligned, the easier it is.

THE UNIVERSE WILL ASSIST. TRUST.

BECOME WHOLE

I have had a full and varied life. My soul has pushed me to achieve as much as possible in this lifetime. I have never really fitted in. I've always worked for myself in various sectors and am great in my own company, but I feel more whole now than I ever have and this is a comment I also hear from my clients.

I can't say it's been easy, but life never really is otherwise we wouldn't learn anything but I can say having mastered the tools I teach, I find it much easier to navigate life's sometimes bumpy road. I'm in flow.

WILL THE PLAN WORK?

If it does, wonderful. If it doesn't, there is a lesson and treasure to be had. Both are equally nourishing to the soul. I guess you could call this equanimity, a certain calmness and non-attachment to the outcome, but with the belief all is coming is key.

The outcome I describe comes by doing the steps leading up to this, to remember fully who you are. Once this work is done, you attract the vibration you are emitting which makes life less of a struggle. We are all going to need this.

I will do my very best to help as many people as possible in the coming months and years ahead. This I know is why I am here.

I trust my teaching has helped and inspired you to find a different way to live. It has been my absolute pleasure to help you heal and grow whether it's during the COVID 19 pandemic or in future years.

Do the work, it's worth it. When you have finished the steps I outline, please carry on good practice. Daily meditation, reading, journaling, helping others, staying in the moment and keeping a close eye on the mind are all on-going tasks, but they won't feel like tasks they will just be new habits that make you feel good.

WE ARE ENERGY BEINGS HAVING A TEMPORARY EXPERIENCE.

WORK WITH ME.

I offer a range of services which are available to view and book on my website.
www.whoamilondon.com

- One to One In person or via zoom
- TEACH THERAPY - One hour call
- Soul Plan Reading
- Depressed to Happy Book
- WAI ON DEMAND 10 lesson programme.
- Corporate Team Mentoring
- Public Speaking
- Retreats - Details coming soon.

I love feedback. You can contact me directly through my website or on socials. If you enjoyed this book please leave a comment on Amazon to help others find me.

It has been my pleasure to assist you at this time and I wish you LOVE, abundance, peace and joy.

NAMASTE

Another world is not only possible she is on her way,

On a quiet day you can hear her breathing.

Arundhati Roy

www.whoamilondon.com

Facebook @who.am.i.london
Instagram @who.am.i.london
Author Charlie Greig
The Teacher
WHO AM I?

Made in the USA
Monee, IL
13 June 2020